P9-DUE-801

WELCOME! ENTER!

PREPARE TO BE DAZZLED!

WALKER & COM

PRESEN

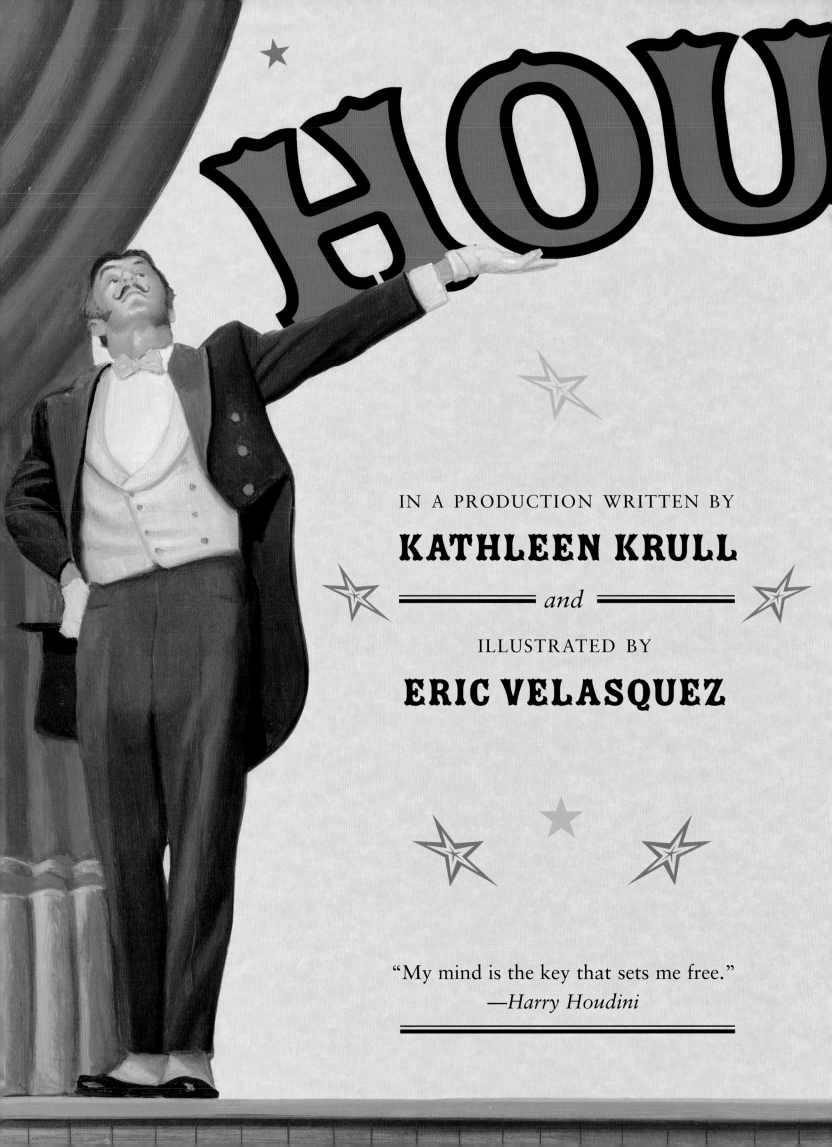

HOU

IN A PRODUCTION WRITTEN BY

KATHLEEN KRULL

and

ILLUSTRATED BY

ERIC VELASQUEZ

"My mind is the key that sets me free."
—*Harry Houdini*

ADA COMMUNITY LIBRARY
10664 W. VICTORY
BOISE, ID 83709

Bright futures begin
with summer reading!

Brought to you by your
library and Read to Me,
a service of
the Idaho
Commission for
Libraries.

Read
to Me

Funding provided by the U.S.
Institute of Museum and Library
Services under the Library Services
and Technology Act.

WORLD'S GREATEST
MYSTERY MAN
— AND —
ESCAPE KING

WALKER & COMPANY ✷ NEW YORK

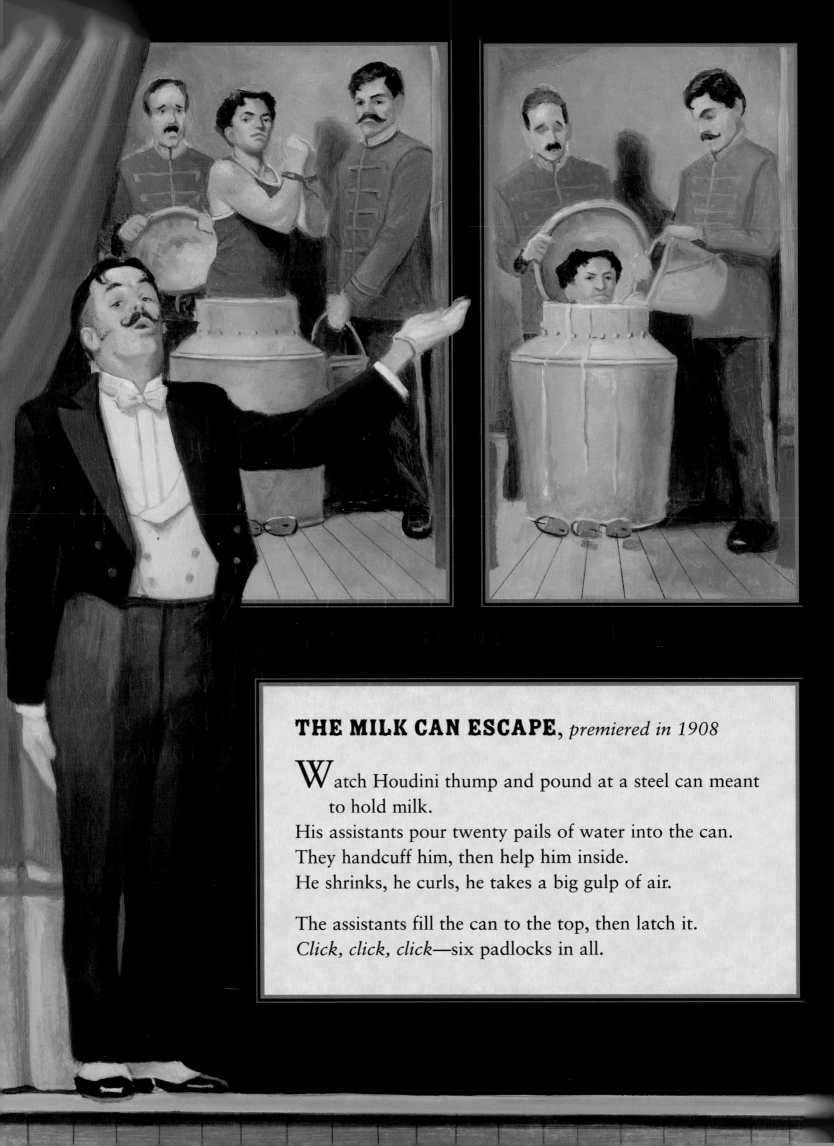

THE MILK CAN ESCAPE, *premiered in 1908*

Watch Houdini thump and pound at a steel can meant
 to hold milk.
His assistants pour twenty pails of water into the can.
They handcuff him, then help him inside.
He shrinks, he curls, he takes a big gulp of air.

The assistants fill the can to the top, then latch it.
Click, click, click—six padlocks in all.

The curtain closes. Now, hold your breath!
Can you hold it for as long as Houdini?
Thirty seconds . . . One minute . . .

Tick, tick, tick—lungs ready to burst.
Failure to escape means a drowning death!
An assistant stands by with an ax just in case.

Just over two minutes.
Behold our Houdini, wet, breathless—but alive!

W ho *was* this man?
Ah, but Houdini was a mystery.
As boggling as his performances.
His journey was epic—
and so were the tales he told about it.

He was born Erik Weiss in Budapest, Hungary, in 1874 (we think). But all his life, he claimed Appleton, Wisconsin, as his hometown. Appleton, with its university, Lawrence College, was on the map for speakers and entertainers, traveling magicians, the circus. It also had a river—the Fox—where Erik swam and got strong.

His father, a scholarly Jewish rabbi, was unsuccessful at earning money. His wife and seven children were always hungry and on the edge of homelessness. Houdini later wrote, "The less said on the subject, the better."

Erik grew up during a time when poor children worked instead of going to school. By age eight he was shining shoes, selling newspapers, running errands, and trying to think up things he could do that others couldn't. He perfected a trapeze act and performed in his backyard as "Prince of the Air." He charged money, of course. But the gasps and applause from the audience were worth almost more than money.

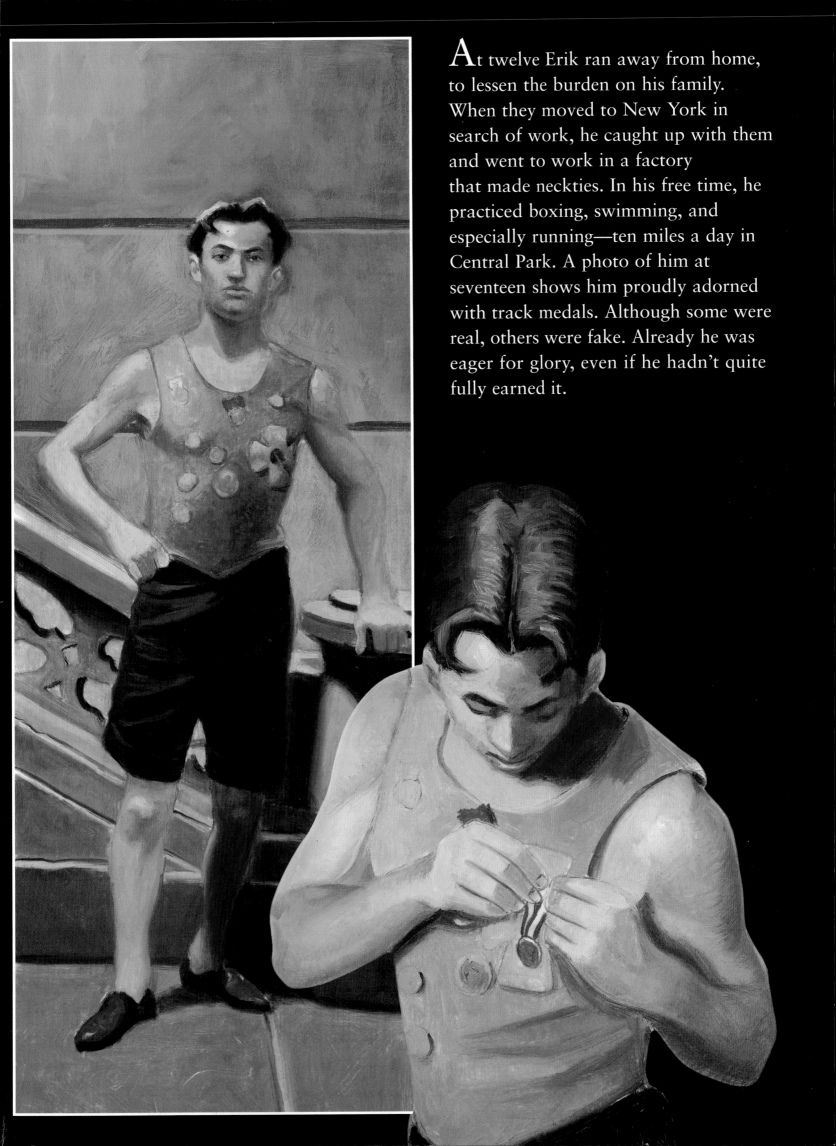

At twelve Erik ran away from home, to lessen the burden on his family. When they moved to New York in search of work, he caught up with them and went to work in a factory that made neckties. In his free time, he practiced boxing, swimming, and especially running—ten miles a day in Central Park. A photo of him at seventeen shows him proudly adorned with track medals. Although some were real, others were fake. Already he was eager for glory, even if he hadn't quite fully earned it.

Houdini's journey to fame really started with a book. Always a big reader, he haunted used bookstores. One day he found a book about the life of the French founder of modern magic.

He memorized this book and became obsessed with magic. He even changed his identity in honor of his hero—whose name was Jean-Eugène Robert-Houdin.

The new Houdini traveled forth, putting on some twelve shows a day—juggling and performing card tricks and magic routines he learned from books. The shows lacked a certain something. But by age nineteen, he was sending precious money home to his beloved mother. And he married Bess Rahner, who was part of a traveling song-and-dance act. She was the love of his life, and her tiny size (less than five feet tall) made her a perfect partner in his first masterpiece, called the Metamorphosis.

THE METAMORPHOSIS, *premiered in 1894*

A curtain opens.
Behold Houdini bound with ropes, placed inside
   a bag, and locked inside a trunk.
   He rocks the trunk, shouting "Let me out!"

   Behold Mrs. Houdini standing in front
      of the open curtain.
   She claps her hands three times, closes
      the curtain.
   Then vanishes.

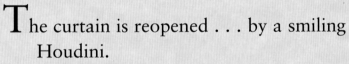

The curtain is reopened . . . by a smiling
    Houdini.
He unlocks the trunk.
Inside, in the same bag and ropes, is little
    Mrs. Houdini!

This trick may sound ordinary.
But the important part is that the switch took
    exactly *three* seconds.
Bess's size meant she could move extra quickly.
Audiences were sometimes too stunned to applaud.

Bess helped Houdini with everything—they were just two people "roaming around trying to make an honest million," he would say. For now, customers paid ten cents.

Over the next six very tough years, Houdini developed one goal: to pack the house. Nothing was more important than warm bodies in a theater—and then keeping them on the edge of their seats.

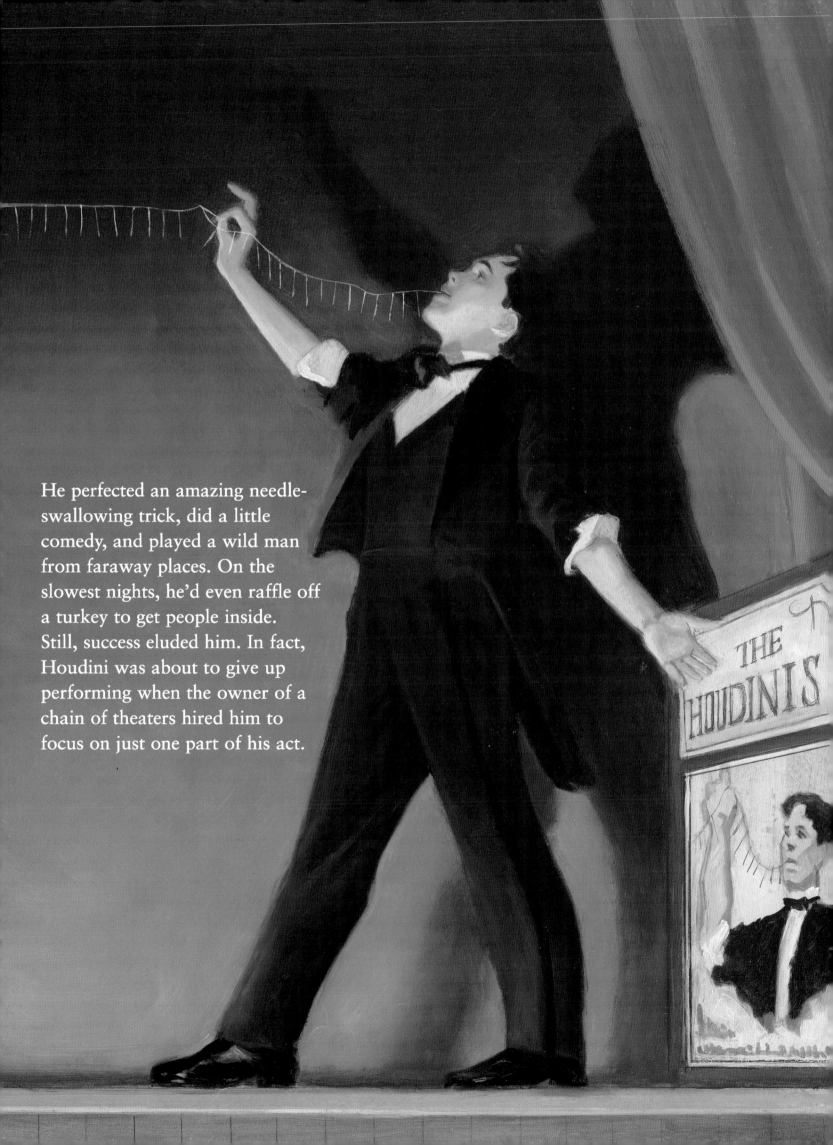

He perfected an amazing needle-swallowing trick, did a little comedy, and played a wild man from faraway places. On the slowest nights, he'd even raffle off a turkey to get people inside. Still, success eluded him. In fact, Houdini was about to give up performing when the owner of a chain of theaters hired him to focus on just one part of his act.

Dramatic escapes brought people into theaters. And Houdini had figured out how to escape from just about every lock ever made. He learned to make his first stop in any town the police station. With reporters present, he'd have the police lock him up in their best handcuffs, or even in a jail cell. He would slither free in minutes. No one knew how. The publicity from the dazzled reporters would guarantee an audience that night.

Houdini's new act billed him as the man who could escape from anything. Soon he was earning four hundred dollars a week, more than most families could earn in a year. With any extra money, he bought more books on magic.

Houdini was a small man—about five feet five inches tall—but unbelievably strong from acrobatics, biking, running, swimming, and playing baseball. When teaching himself something new, he would practice six, seven, eight hours a day. And in squirming out of straitjackets and all sorts of tight spots, Houdini decided that his worst enemy was not physical danger but panic. So he practiced the hardest at conquering fear— of the dark, the pain, lack of air, the cold.

By this point he was becoming famous for his thrilling performances. Then he started jumping off bridges.

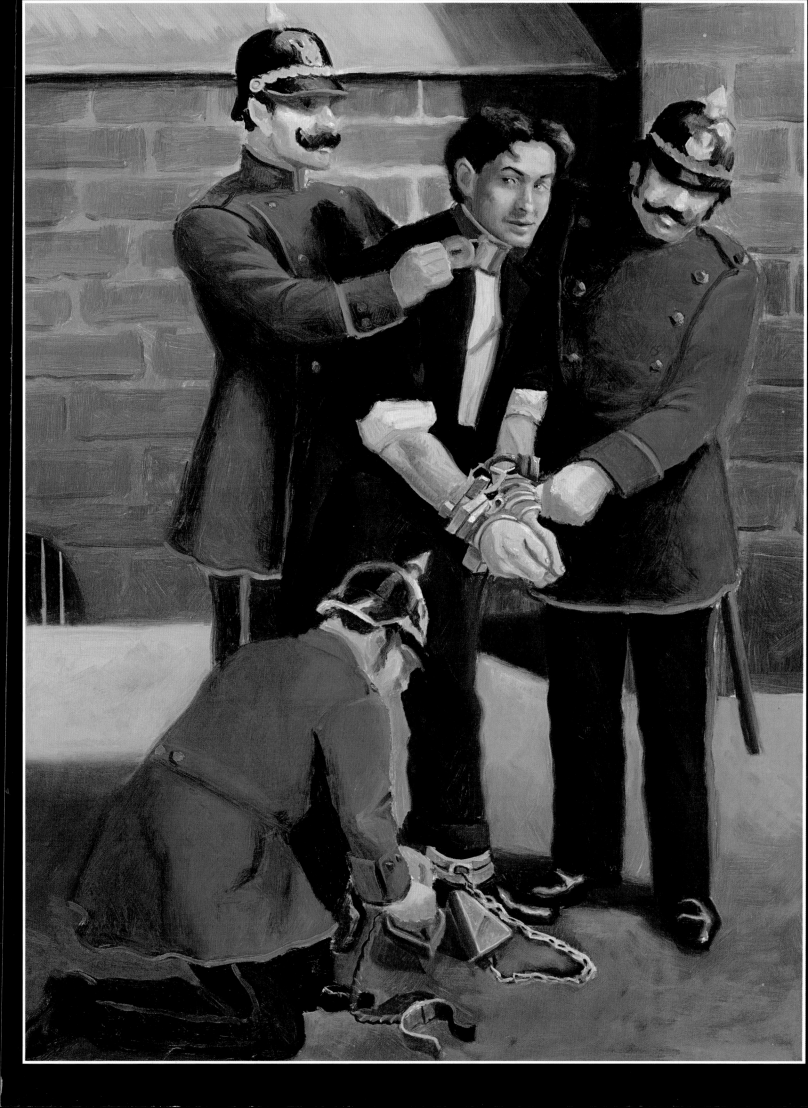

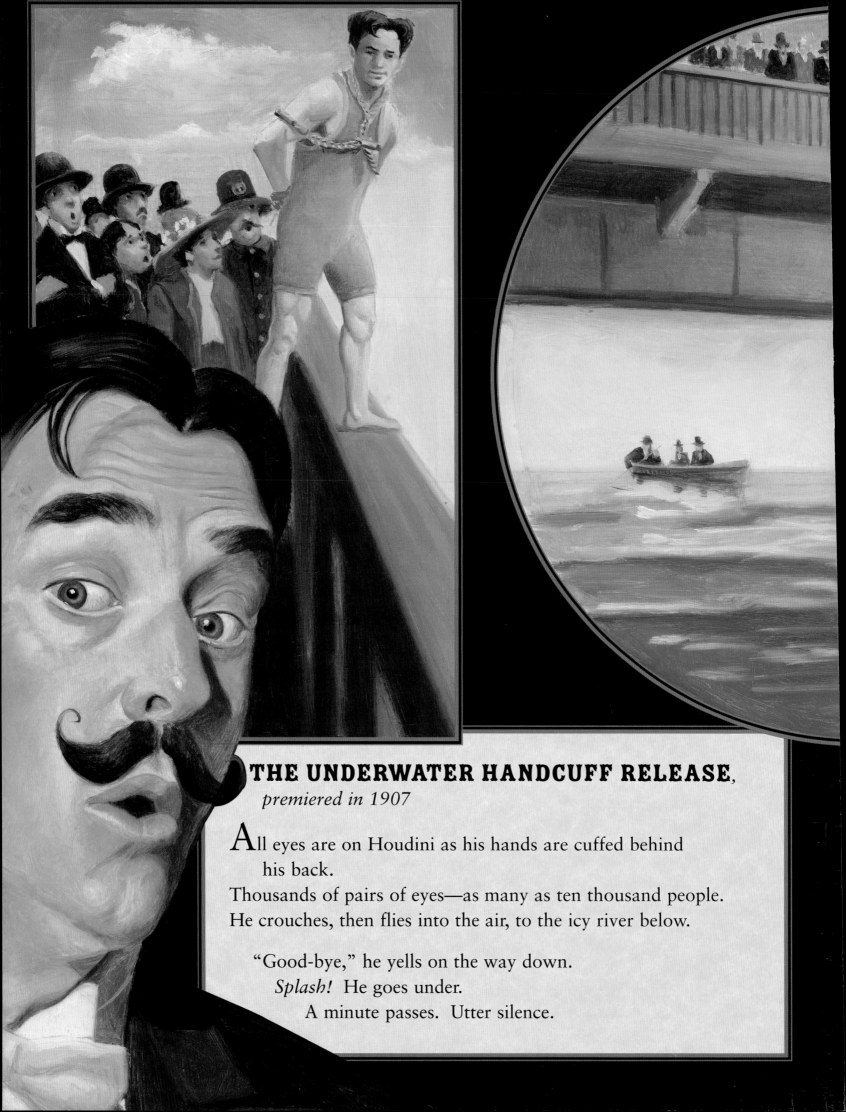

THE UNDERWATER HANDCUFF RELEASE, *premiered in 1907*

All eyes are on Houdini as his hands are cuffed behind
  his back.
Thousands of pairs of eyes—as many as ten thousand people.
He crouches, then flies into the air, to the icy river below.

"Good-bye," he yells on the way down.
  Splash! He goes under.
    A minute passes. Utter silence.

Houdini pops up, his hands free, waving in triumph.
The crowd roars, absolutely hysterical!

There was no way to charge money for a bridge jump, of course.
But the publicity *never failed* to sell out that night's show.
If you saw one of his outdoor performances, you talked
        about it all day.
You talked about it for the rest of your life.

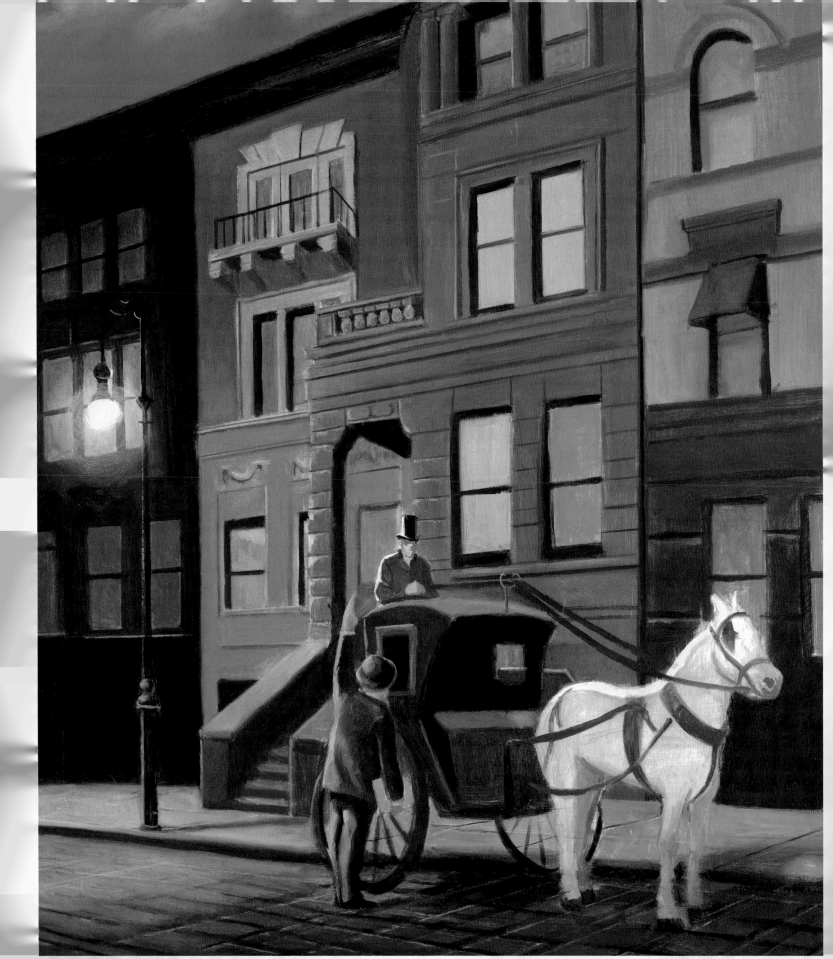

H e installed a huge sunken bathtub, in which he practiced such escape tricks
as the Milk Can. He trained himself to hold his breath underwater for minutes at a
time. Into the tub he slid blocks of ice, noting in his diary: On Monday he could
tolerate 52 degrees. . . . Tuesday, down to 48 . . . then 36 . . .

Houdini took in and supported his whole family. In the morning he left mushy
love notes on Bess's pillow. They were unhappy that they had no children, but
their relationship was playful.

Most important, he now had a home for his books. Floor-to-ceiling bookshelves
lined the walls. "I actually live in a library," he boasted. It was the largest library of
magic in America, and eventually Houdini hired a librarian to work for him full-time.

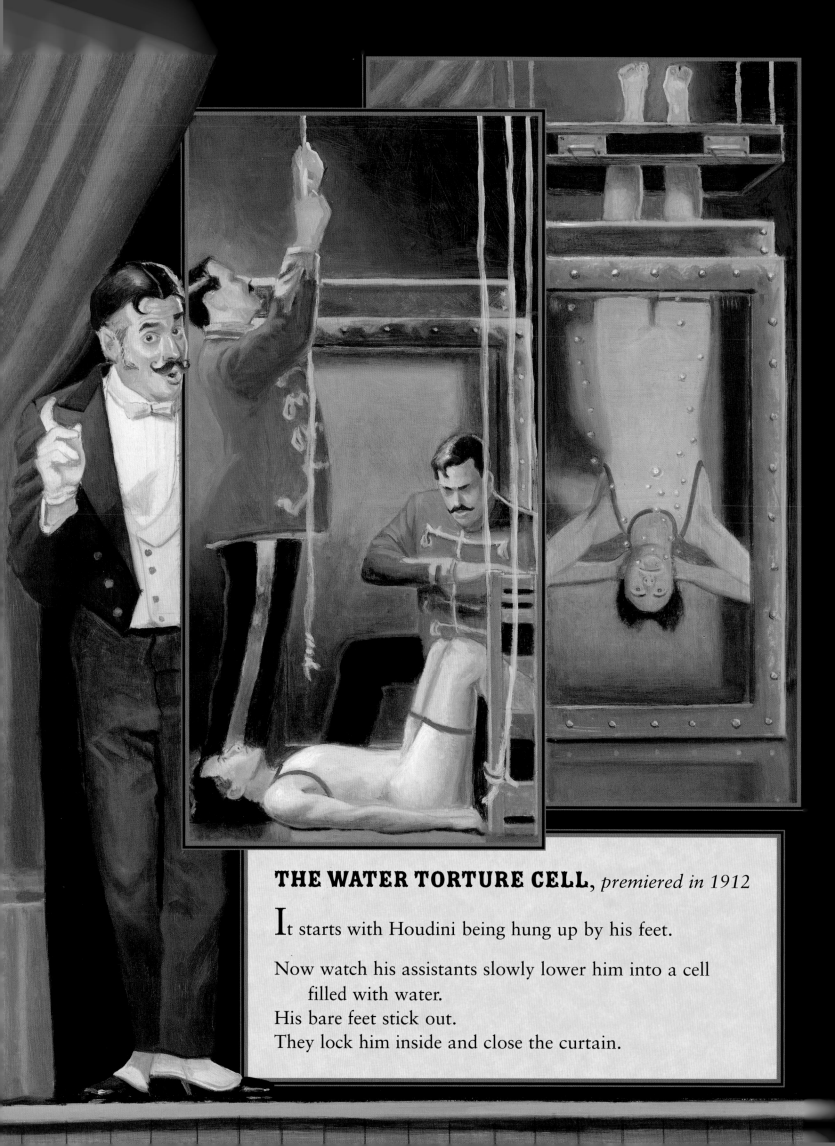

THE WATER TORTURE CELL, *premiered in 1912*

It starts with Houdini being hung up by his feet.

Now watch his assistants slowly lower him into a cell
   filled with water.
His bare feet stick out.
They lock him inside and close the curtain.

Underwater and upside down he hangs.
He cannot breathe.
A wrong move will break an ankle.

But he always makes the right moves—
and people weep openly with relief.

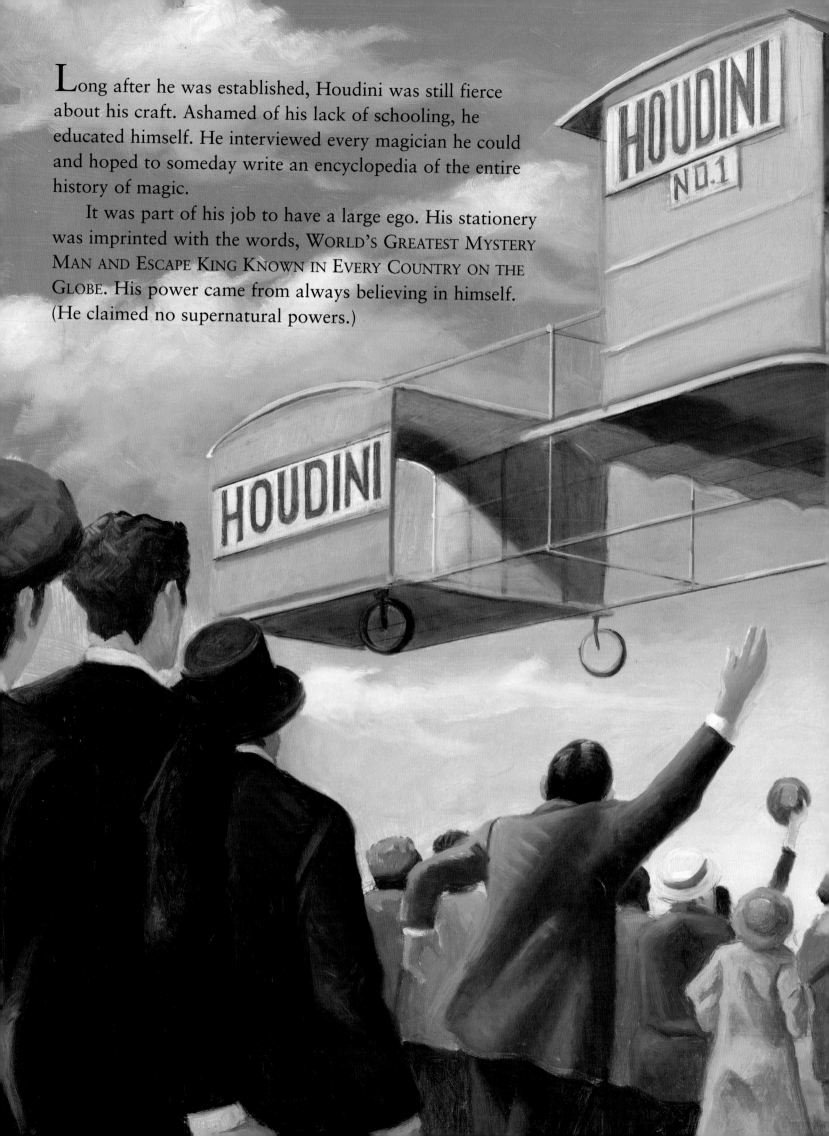

Long after he was established, Houdini was still fierce about his craft. Ashamed of his lack of schooling, he educated himself. He interviewed every magician he could and hoped to someday write an encyclopedia of the entire history of magic.

It was part of his job to have a large ego. His stationery was imprinted with the words, WORLD'S GREATEST MYSTERY MAN AND ESCAPE KING KNOWN IN EVERY COUNTRY ON THE GLOBE. His power came from always believing in himself. (He claimed no supernatural powers.)

Houdini had a big heart. He loved children and often performed free for those in hospitals and orphanages. Late in life he went around unmasking performers he thought were cheating the public.

Houdini also had a knack for changing with the times. He took up flying and became the first person to fly in Australia. He plunged into moviemaking (though not successfully, because audiences knew tricks could easily be faked on-screen). As skyscrapers began rising, full of offices for brand-new kinds of businesses, Houdini simply used the tall buildings in his act.

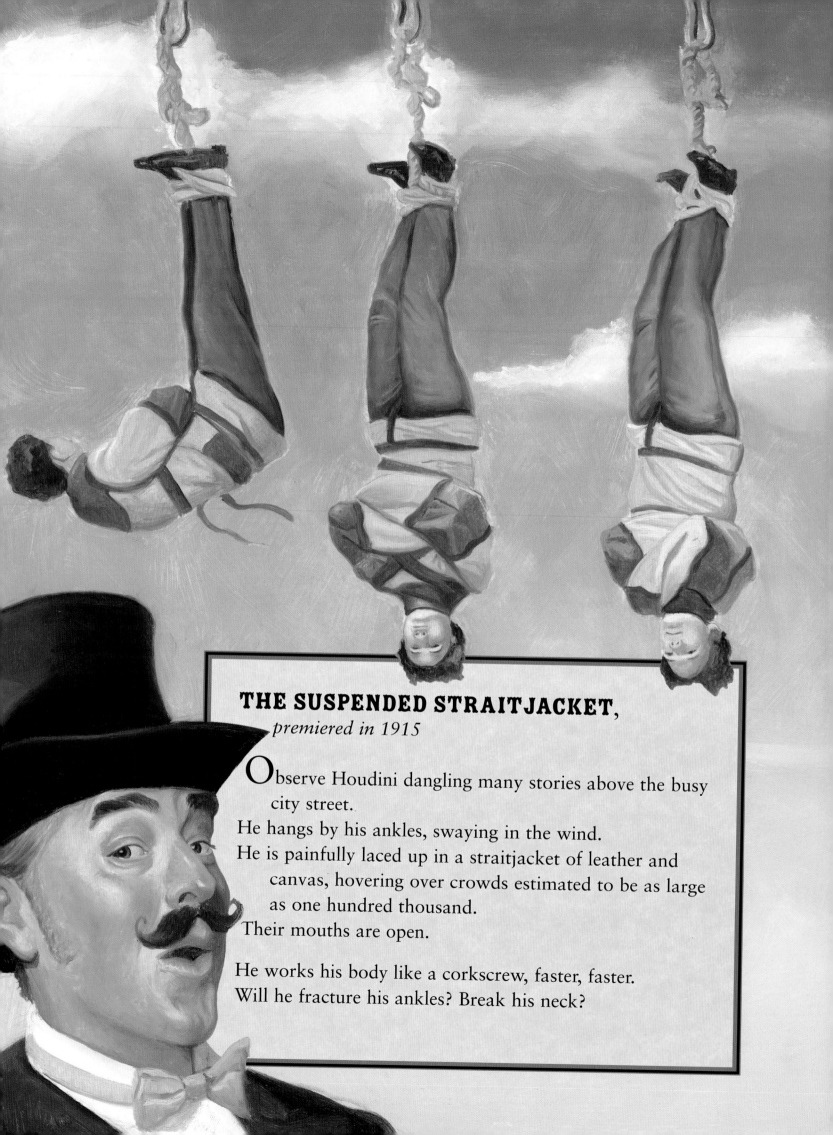

THE SUSPENDED STRAITJACKET,
premiered in 1915

Observe Houdini dangling many stories above the busy city street.

He hangs by his ankles, swaying in the wind.

He is painfully laced up in a straitjacket of leather and canvas, hovering over crowds estimated to be as large as one hundred thousand.

Their mouths are open.

He works his body like a corkscrew, faster, faster.

Will he fracture his ankles? Break his neck?

A vast sea of faces looks up, worried.
He frees one arm, then the other.
At last he holds up the jacket, then drops it to the
    fans below.

His grin is upside down, but so wide that every person
    can see it.

Houdini was finally "Prince of the Air,"
    just as he predicted as a child.
He performed this escape in every town he visited over
    the next ten years.
It was the greatest triumph of a triumphant life.

AND WE TRULY HOPE YOU
ENJOYED HIS SHOW!!!

BEHIND THE SCENES

Houdini died at age fifty-two, on Halloween, 1926. It didn't happen during one of his escapes, after all. He had been performing despite a fractured ankle and appendicitis. When he allowed a college student to punch him in the stomach to test his muscles, his appendix burst, spreading an infection throughout his body. He died within days.

The most important part of being a magician is that you NEVER tell your secrets. Houdini didn't tell. But we know a few things.

He had the ability to expand his chest while being tied up. So, when escaping from a straitjacket, for example, he would deflate his chest and shoulders, work his arms up and over his head, and with his arms free, unbuckle the back of the jacket.

Getting one hand or foot free was always the first step in an escape, he once revealed. He would spit on his wrists before being bound, to make them slippery, and would wear shoes with no laces—they were easier to kick off (plus keys could be hidden inside them).

Houdini's muscle control was extraordinary. He could pick up a coin with his palm. He trained his toes to work as efficiently as fingers. (He was also known to use his teeth.) He even used his throat muscles—he learned how to swallow small objects and bring them back up. (He practiced with small potatoes at first . . . just in case.)

His research was notoriously obsessive. When studying locks, he collected every kind that he could find. He pulled them apart and memorized how they worked. (That's how he learned that most could be opened with just a few basic keys or even a sharp tap to a certain place.) "I know more about locks and how to work them than any man living," he once stated.

He practiced relentlessly before performing an escape on stage—for months with the Milk Can. He practiced the Water Torture Cell for more than *three years* before performing it in public.

He polished his acting, becoming a pro at misdirecting an audience's attention—what magicians do best—and making things look more difficult than they really were.

But he was often in genuine danger. Sometimes he did suffer minor injuries or emerge from an escape bloody and swollen. Several times he was led off a stage

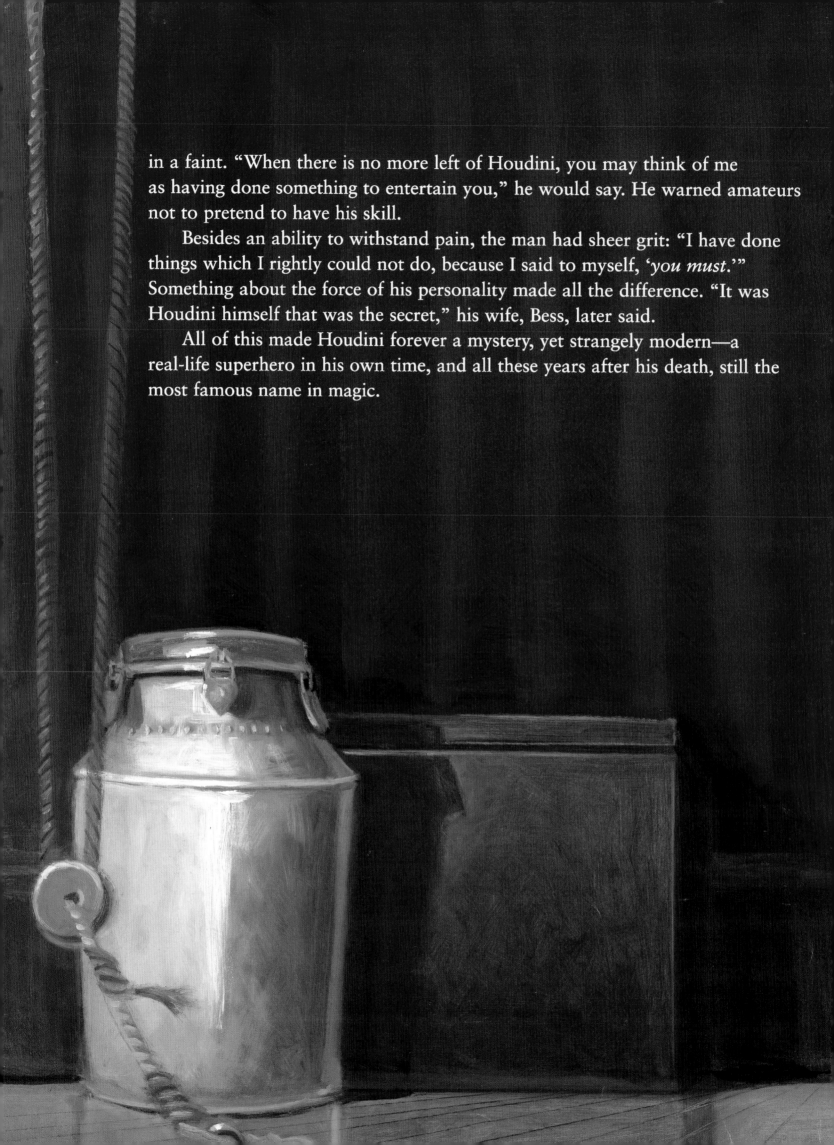

in a faint. "When there is no more left of Houdini, you may think of me as having done something to entertain you," he would say. He warned amateurs not to pretend to have his skill.

Besides an ability to withstand pain, the man had sheer grit: "I have done things which I rightly could not do, because I said to myself, *'you must.'*" Something about the force of his personality made all the difference. "It was Houdini himself that was the secret," his wife, Bess, later said.

All of this made Houdini forever a mystery, yet strangely modern—a real-life superhero in his own time, and all these years after his death, still the most famous name in magic.

BIBLIOGRAPHY

Randi, Amazing, and Bert Randolph Sugar. *Houdini: His Life and Art*. New York: Grosset & Dunlap, 1976.

Cannell, J. C. *The Secrets of Houdini*. New York: Dover, 1973.

Cox, Clinton. *Houdini: Master of Illusion*. New York: Scholastic, 2001.

Henning, Doug, with Charles Reynolds. *Houdini: His Legend and His Magic*. New York: Warner Books, 1977.

Kasson, John F. *Houdini, Tarzan, and the Perfect Man*. New York: Hill and Wang, 2001.

Lalicki, Tom. *Spellbinder: The Life of Harry Houdini*. New York: Holiday House, 2000.

Silverman, Kenneth. *Houdini!!! The Career of Ehrich Weiss*. New York: HarperCollins, 1996.

Sutherland, Tui T. *Who Was Harry Houdini?* New York: Grosset & Dunlap, 2002.

OTHER SOURCES

Houdini, the PBS American Experience film. http://www.pbs.org/wgbh/amex/houdini/ (accessed March 29, 2004).

Houdini Historical Center, Appleton, Wisconsin. http://www.foxvalleyhistory.org/houdini/ (accessed March 29, 2004).

Library of Congress. "American Memory" collection of Houdini Photographs and Memorabilia. http:/lcweb2.loc.gov/ammem/vshtml/vshdini.html (accessed March 29, 2004).

TO THE HOUDINIS OF WINFIELD, ILLINOIS—ALLISON AND BRIAN. —K. K.

FOR THE MOST MAGICAL EDITOR, EMILY EASTON. —E. V.

Text copyright © 2005 by Kathleen Krull
Illustrations copyright © 2005 by Eric Velasquez

All rights reserved. No part of this book may be reproduced or transmitted in any form or by any means, electronic or mechanical, including photocopying, recording, or by any information storage and retrieval system, without permission in writing from the Publisher.

First published in the United States of America in 2005 by Walker Publishing Company, Inc.

Distributed to the trade by Holtzbrinck Publishers

For information about permission to reproduce selections from this book, write to Permissions, Walker & Company, 104 Fifth Avenue, New York, New York 10011

Library of Congress Cataloging-in-Publication Data
Krull, Kathleen.
Houdini : world's greatest mystery man and escape king / in a production
written by Kathleen Krull ; illustrated by Eric Velasquez.
    p. cm.
Includes bibliographical references.
ISBN 0-8027-8953-6 — ISBN 0-8027-8954-4 (lib. bdg.)
 1. Houdini, Harry, 1874-1926—Juvenile literature. 2. Magicians—United States—Biography—Juvenile literature.
3. Magicians—United States—Pictorial works—Juvenile literature. 4. Escape artists—United States—Biography—
Juvenile literature. 5. Escape artists—United States—Pictorial works—Juvenile literature. I. Title: Houdini. II.
Velasquez, Eric, ill. III. Title.

GV1545.H8K73 2005
793.8'092—dc22
[B]
2004049493

The illustrations for this book were created using oil paint on Fabriano Artistico watercolor paper.

Book design by Victoria Allen

Visit Walker & Company's Web site at www.walkeryoungreaders.com

Printed in China

10 9 8 7 6 5 4 3 2